THE ART OF MINDFULNESS

MINDFUL CRAFTING

BY STEPHANIE FINNE

BLUE OWL
BOOKS

TIPS FOR CAREGIVERS

Social and emotional learning (SEL) helps children manage emotions, create and achieve goals, maintain relationships, learn how to feel empathy, and make good decisions. The SEL approach will help children establish positive habits in communication, cooperation, and decision-making. By incorporating SEL in early reading, children will be better equipped to build confidence and foster positive peer networks.

BEFORE READING

Talk to the reader about what he or she enjoys about crafting.

Discuss: How do you feel when you make something creative?
What is the part you enjoy most?

AFTER READING

Talk to the reader about how being creative helps him or her be mindful.

Discuss: How does creating art help you stay in the present moment?
Do you find it easier to focus after doing something creative?

SEL GOAL

Some students may struggle with anxiety, making it hard to regulate their emotions, thoughts, and behaviors. Help readers develop these skills by learning to slow down and tune into their minds and bodies. Crafting can help readers slow down, focus on the present, and control their breathing.

TABLE OF CONTENTS

CHAPTER 1

WHY GET CRAFTY?

Mindfulness means being in the present moment. When you are mindful, you pay attention to how your mind and body feel. One way to practice mindfulness is to be creative.

Crafting is creative. It requires you to **focus**. When you focus on creating art, you slow down and listen to your mind and body.

CHAPTER 2

LET'S CRAFT MINDFULLY!

The first step to crafting mindfully is setting your **intention**. What are you choosing to craft, and why?

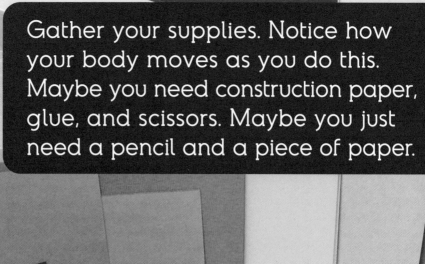

Gather your supplies. Notice how your body moves as you do this. Maybe you need construction paper, glue, and scissors. Maybe you just need a pencil and a piece of paper.

HELPFUL HINT: When drawing, watch how the pencil moves. Feel how your hand moves.

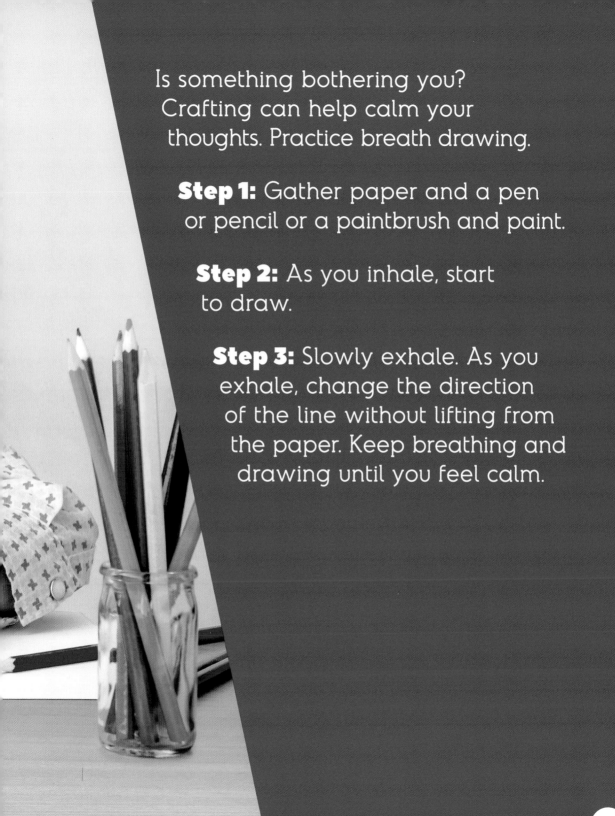

Is something bothering you? Crafting can help calm your thoughts. Practice breath drawing.

Step 1: Gather paper and a pen or pencil or a paintbrush and paint.

Step 2: As you inhale, start to draw.

Step 3: Slowly exhale. As you exhale, change the direction of the line without lifting from the paper. Keep breathing and drawing until you feel calm.

Crafting can help you focus on what is happening right now. Taking photos is one way to stay present. Look through the camera lens to see the world in a different way. Pay attention to what is happening around you. What do you notice?

CRAFTING WITH PHOTOS

Look through your photos. Choose some that make you happy or remind you of a good feeling. Ask an adult to help you print them. Paste them into an album or a scrapbook, or decorate them with sayings or stickers.

HELPFUL HINT: Zooming in can make photos blurry. Get close to your subject. This will keep your photos sharp!

vision
board

dream
BIG

work hard

play hard

You can craft as a way to set **goals** and **inspire** yourself. Vision boards help do this, and they're fun to make!

Step 1: Gather a large posterboard, magazines, scissors, markers, and stickers.

Step 2: Find pictures and words that inspire you and show your goals. Add them to your board and decorate it as you like.

Step 3: Place your vision board somewhere you will see it often. It will help inspire you to work toward your goals.

A mind jar can help you pay attention to both your mind and body.

Step 1: Find a small, clear jar. Fill it most of the way with water.

Step 2: Add a few spoonfuls of glitter glue. If you have loose glitter, add that, too.

Step 3: Screw the lid on tight, shake the jar, and watch the glitter swirl. Focus on slowing your breathing as you watch the glitter settle.

SWIRLING THOUGHTS

When the glitter swirls, it is like your thoughts when you are angry or sad. It can be hard to think clearly. Let the glitter settle at the bottom. The water becomes clear and is easy to see through. This is what happens in your mind when you are calm.

mind jar

HELPFUL HINT: Fill the jar halfway with warm water. Then add cold water. This will keep the glitter from clumping.

mandala ·····▶

HELPFUL HINT: If your mind wanders, come back to the center of the circle.

Notice your senses as you craft. Creating a **mandala** is one way to do this.

Step 1: Gather rocks, shells, flowers, or leaves from outside.

Step 2: Start the mandala at its center. Using the items you gathered, create a pattern moving outward.

Step 3: Pay attention to how the items feel. What are their **textures**? How do they smell?

CHAPTER 3

ADMIRING YOUR MASTERPIECE

Creating art can be something you do just for you. You can be messy or **precise**. You can use a lot of colors or just a few. It is up to you!

After making your craft, **reflect** on how it went. Did you stay focused? Did you enjoy being creative? How did it make you feel?

When crafting mindfully, the **process** is the important part. Don't worry about how the craft turned out. It is beautiful because you worked hard on it!

NO JUDGMENT ZONE

Think about your feelings as you create. As with your art, try not to judge if a feeling is good or bad. **Accept** the feeling. Stay in the present.

GOALS AND TOOLS

GROW WITH GOALS

Crafting mindfully can help you stay in the present moment. Work on these goals:

Goal: Focus on your breathing as you move through the steps of the craft.

Goal: Tune into all your senses as you create your masterpiece.

Goal: Look at what you've created without judgment. Everything you create is special.

TRY THIS!

Make a worry box. This is a container that can hold your worries so you can focus on other things.

1. Find a box or container, such as a shoebox or tissue box. Gather materials to decorate the box. Pick materials and colors that bring you joy. These could be stickers, magazine cutouts, or glitter.

2. Decorate the box however you like. Write or create a label that reads "Worry Box."

3. Tear or cut up slips of paper. Leave the slips and a pen or pencil near the box.

4. Whenever you have a worry, write it on a slip of paper. Put the paper in the box. The box can hold your worry for you so that you can focus on other things.

GLOSSARY

accept
To agree that something is correct, satisfactory, or enough.

crafting
Skillfully making things with your hands.

focus
To concentrate on something.

goals
Things you aim to do.

inspire
To influence and encourage someone to achieve or do something.

intention
Something you mean to do.

mandala
A geometric design made up of symbols that can be used to focus one's attention.

mindfulness
A mentality achieved by focusing on the present moment and calmly recognizing and accepting your feelings, thoughts, and sensations.

precise
Very neat and careful about details.

process
A series of actions or steps that create something.

reflect
To think carefully or seriously about something.

textures
The ways things feel, especially how rough or smooth they are.

TO LEARN MORE

FACT SURFER

Finding more information is as easy as 1, 2, 3.

1. Go to www.factsurfer.com

2. Enter "**mindfulcrafting**" into the search box.

3. Choose your book to see a list of websites.

INDEX

Blue Owl Books are published by Jump!, 5357 Penn Avenue South, Minneapolis, MN 55419, www.jumplibrary.com

Copyright © 2022 Jump! International copyright reserved in all countries. No part of this book may be reproduced in any form without written permission from the publisher.

Library of Congress Cataloging-in-Publication Data

Names: Finne, Stephanie, author.
Title: Mindful crafting / by Stephanie Finne.
Description: Minneapolis: Jump!, Inc., [2022]
Series: The art of mindfulness | Includes index. | Audience: Ages 7–10
Identifiers: LCCN 2021030854 (print)
LCCN 2021030855 (ebook)
ISBN 9781636903613 (hardcover)
ISBN 9781636903620 (paperback)
ISBN 9781636903637 (ebook)
Subjects: LCSH: Handicraft for children–Juvenile literature. | Mindfulness (Psychology)–Juvenile literature.
Classification: LCC TT160 .F535 2022 (print) | LCC TT160 (ebook) | DDC 745.5083–dc23
LC record available at https://lccn.loc.gov/2021030854
LC ebook record available at https://lccn.loc.gov/2021030855

Editor: Jenna Gleisner
Designer: Michelle Sonnek

Photo Credits: Shutterstock, cover, 12–13; Spiderstock/iStock, 1; studiovin/Shutterstock, 3; tanaphongpict/Shutterstock, 4; Lena May/Shutterstock, 5; PeopleImages/iStock, 6; zefirchik06/Shutterstock, 7; Joyseulay/Shutterstock, 8–9; Marcus Lindstrom/iStock, 10–11; Dorling Kindersley ltd/Alamy, 14–15; Natalia Lebedinskaia/Shutterstock, 16–17; New Africa/Shutterstock, 18; Krakenimages.com/Shutterstock, 19; Bhupi/iStock, 20–21.

Printed in the United States of America at Corporate Graphics in North Mankato, Minnesota.